Published in Great Britain 1996
by Bloomsbury Children's Books
2 Soho Square, London W1V 6HB

Copyright © 1996 Caroline Plaisted
Illustrations © 1996 Clive Scruton

The moral rights of the author and
illustrator have been asserted.

A CIP catalogue record for this book
is available from the British Library.

ISBN 0-7475-2624-9
10 9 8 7 6 5 4 3 2 1

Printed and bound in Britain
by Cox & Wyman Ltd, Reading, Berkshire

THE GOLDFISH ATE MY KNICKERS!

The Best Book of Excuses Ever

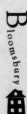

A Bloomsbury Paperback Original

The Goldfish
Ate My Knickers!

I always seem to be in trouble. Whether it's because I've turned up for school wearing a Gladiators outfit instead of my uniform, called my brother's latest girlfriend by the name of the one before or spilt purple ink all over my gran's white sofa . . . That's why I've become so good at excuses.

In fact, I know so many excuses that I thought I could earn some extra pocket money by putting all my experience into this, the **Best Book of Excuses Ever**. (After all, I always need extra cash.)

Then, this morning, the most terrible thing happened. I jumped out of bed, ready to start writing this introduction when . . . *I couldn't find my knickers!* I looked everywhere — and then I spotted it: a little bit of knicker elastic, dangling from the mouth of my goldfish. It was *my* knicker elastic, from *my* knickers. Because, you see, the goldfish had taken a fancy to my new knickers, leaped out of its bowl and ate them! Yes, **the goldfish ate my knickers**!

So I didn't have time to write any more introduction . . .

Why You Need This Book

Even if you think you're an expert at excuses too, you can never have enough. And you need especially clever ones to get you out of serious trouble with Found U Out — that well-known goody two-shoes who's in league with everybody's parents to get you into bother.

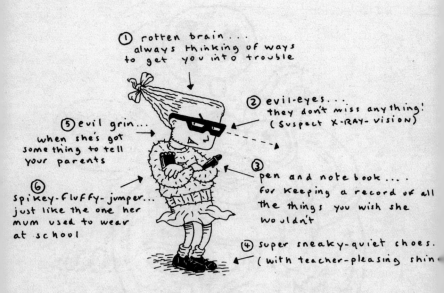

1 rotten brain...
always thinking of ways to get you into trouble

2 evil-eyes...
they don't miss anything!
(suspect X-RAY-VISION)

5 evil grin...
when she's got something to tell your parents

3 pen and notebook....
for keeping a record of all the things you wish she wouldn't

6 spikey-fluffy-jumper...
just like the one her mum used to wear at school

4 super sneaky-quiet choes.
(with teacher-pleasing shin

Have you kicked your brother's new football into the canal? Have you fused your sister's electric hair curlers by trying them out on the dog? Was it you who used your mum's Chanel lipstick as Indian warpaint? Unless you've thought of a very good excuse indeed, Found U Out will find you out.

I've tried to keep her out of this book, but it just wasn't possible. I've been too busy shopping for new underwear.

Contents

Are You an Absolute Angel or Has Your Halo Slipped?

Test your skills at making decisions and excuses in these sticky situations. Keep a record of your choices — and then see what Found U Out has to say about you at the end of the quiz.

1   YOU'VE WOKEN UP LATE! You can:

☐ **a)** skip breakfast and cadge a lift from your dad so that you don't have to get the bus;

☐ **b)** eat breakfast and then walk to the bus stop — after all, it's only five minutes away;

☑ **c)** stay in bed even longer so that you don't need to go to school at all.

2 IT'S YOUR CLASS'S TURN TO DO SCHOOL ASSEMBLY NEXT WEEK. Do you :

☐ **a)** wait for someone else to become the team leader and then give them your support in doing the assembly preparation;

☑ **b)** volunteer to organize the whole thing immediately and impress the Headmaster with your amazing pets;

☐ **c)** keep completely silent – with a bit of luck you won't even be asked to sing with everyone else at the end.

3 YOUR TEACHER HAS ASKED YOU TO DO A PROJECT BY THE END OF TERM.

So you:

☐ **a)** leave it for a few weeks before you start thinking about it and then complete it in a rush;

☐ **b)** go to the library at the earliest opportunity and work hard at the project at least two nights every week until the end of term;

☑ **c)** don't do anything at all until the week before you are due to hand the project in. Then, get the project your brother did last year and copy it in your own handwriting and hand it in at the right time and with a smug smile on your face.

4 YOUR BEST FRIEND HAS ASKED IF S/HE CAN COPY YOUR MATHS HOMEWORK.

Do you:

☐ **a)** say they can copy some as long as they don't give exactly the same answers for every question;

☑ **b)** tell them that they cannot copy your homework on any account;

☐ **c)** let them copy everything – providing they let you copy their maths homework next week.

5 YOU SNEAKED IN TO THE KITCHEN LONG AFTER YOU WERE TOLD TO GO TO BED, TOOK A PIECE OF CHOCOLATE CAKE FROM THE FRIDGE . . . AND GOT CAUGHT BY YOUR DAD. You can:

☐ **a)** tell him that you were getting a packed lunch ready for school tomorrow so that you wouldn't have to rush in the morning;

☐ **b)** admit that you couldn't resist another piece of the scrumptious cake he and mum had made;

☑ **c)** tell him you were actually coming to get a glass of milk and you had to move the cake out of the way before you could reach the milk.

13

6 IT'S YOUR TURN TO HELP GET THE SCHOOL HALL READY FOR ASSEMBLY. Do you:

☐ **a)** wait until your form teacher reminds you before you leave the playground to go and lay all those chairs out in the hall;

☐ **b)** set the alarm on your watch ten minutes earlier than you need to so that you couldn't possibly forget or not have everything ready on time;

☑ **c)** lock yourself in the lavatory until after assembly and when they find out say you couldn't open the door.

7 IT'S YOUR SISTER'S BIRTHDAY AND YOU'VE ONLY JUST REMEMBERED. THE ONLY POCKET MONEY YOU HAVE LEFT IS WHAT YOU SAVED UP TO BUY THE SPECIAL SET OF POGS YOU WANTED FOR YOURSELF. Would you:

☐ **a)** buy the Pogs anyway but share them with your sister;

☐ **b)** give the Pogs to her as a present;

☑ **c)** buy the Pogs, keep them a secret and then tell your sister that the goldfish ate the present you bought her . . .

8 YOUR DAD REMINDS YOU THAT YOU SHOULD BE DOING SOME PIANO PRACTICE BEFORE YOUR NEXT LESSON.

Do you:

☑ **a)** agree to do half an hour of scales, but only if you can stay up late to watch the film on telly on Saturday night;

☐ **b)** rush to the piano immediately and tinkle away on the ivories all evening;

☐ **c)** develop an automatic piano-playing machine to make him think you're practising while you watch TV.

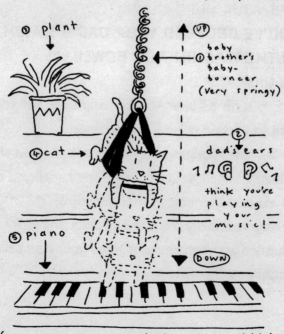

catomatic piano player

① plant

⊕ baby brother's baby-bouncer (very springy)

④ cat →

② dad's ears think you're playing your music! —

⑤ piano

(now you can watch T.V. !!!)

Dad! I am astounded!

9 YOU'VE DROPPED YOUR DAD'S WATCH IN THE WASHING-UP BOWL!

So you:

☑ **a)** dry it off as best you can and then tell your dad you found it lying on the floor;

☐ **b)** tell him straight away what you did and then offer to forfeit your pocket money until you have saved enough money for the repairs;

☐ **c)** keep well away from the kitchen and look stunned with amazement when your dad tells you about the watch.

10 YOUR GRAN TELLS YOU OFF BECAUSE
YOUR AUNTY HAS TOLD HER YOU DIDN'T
SEND A THANK YOU LETTER AFTER SHE
GAVE YOU A BIRTHDAY PRESENT.
Would you:

☐ **a)** say it's been on your conscience and then
write a letter immediately, apologizing and
belatedly thanking her;

☐ **b)** be genuinely horrified – because you sent a
letter the very next day which must have got
lost in the post;

☑ **c)** pretend to be surprised – and tell her that you
sent a letter (even though you know you didn't).

So, are You Really an Angel?

Work out your score from this Excuses Scale:

For every **a)** you chose, score **1 point**;
For every **b)** you chose, score **2 points**;
For every **c)** you chose, score **3 points**.

If you scored 10-15 points:
You don't make too many
excuses which means you
could try a bit harder.
On the other hand, most
of us would probably do the
same thing in your shoes.

❝But I still think it would
be a good idea to read the
rest of the book in case
you do get in trouble.❞

If you scored 16-25 points:

Well, you are obviously very fortunate because you don't sound like you get into enough trouble to need an excuse very often.

"I'd buy some more polish for that halo if I were you!"

If you scored 26-30 points:

Have you got any conscience at all? Why are you reading this book? You've obviously told so many fibs that you probably could have written it yourself!

"You really are a Totally Outrageous Excuses Repetitious Action Goof — in other words a TOERAG!"

Stop the Shop

You don't want to go shopping but your mum and dad think you are in need of some nice winter vests and a 'proper pair of school shoes' instead of your favourite ultra-trendy trainers. The shopping expedition is set for the following weekend. What do you do?

Try the:
QUICK-AS-A-FLASH ANSWER

> *Tell them not to spend their hard-earned cash on you but to give it to charity instead.*

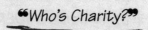
"Who's Charity?"

Can you think of a good excuse not to go shopping?

....

....

Or . . . you've got two options in order to avoid the gruesome, foot-aching experience of a trot around town . . .

OPTION A: Tell your parents that the school nurse has issued a warning of a terrible verruca epidemic. No one, under any circumstances, should even contemplate taking their shoes and socks off in public. Stress to your parents that you feel responsibility as a good citizen to keep the epidemic under control – and point out that someone else, (who doesn't come from such a well brought up family as yours) may well have been around the shoe-shops with a heavily-verrucaed foot, infecting the same footwear that you're just about try on .

(Don't overdo the toadiness or your mum and dad will begin to smell a rat as well as your smelly feet!)

OPTION B: Get the school counterfeiter to write up a list of new school rules which announces that from now on everyone is allowed to wear trainers to school. Present this to your parents the evening before the trip, saying: 'Isn't this great? Now I can wear my old trainers at school and you won't have to spend any extra dosh on another pair.'

(If it works, this excuse will only last until the next parent/teacher meeting when your teacher is bound to ask why you don't wear the regulation school shoes . . .)

❝You slimy toad! What's wrong with wearing a sensible pair of shoes at school and keeping your trendy trainers for best and weekends?❞

❝Some of us manage with a rather smart pair of fins.❞

Sweet Dreams

As a special treat, you were given some particularly yummy sweeties and, rather predictably, despite being told that you should 'make them last for the weekend' you've gone and scoffed the lot. Now your cousin has turned up and your parents have asked you to hand your confectionery collection around . . .

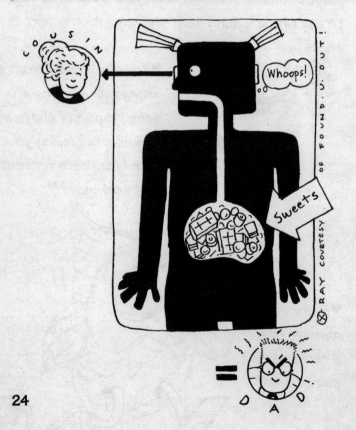

Hmmm. It's probably not the first time that you've chomped your way through pounds of choccies on your own! If you think a quick excuse won't work, it could be time for a **TALL** Story. On this occasion, your lack of tuck is the result of your overwhelming generosity and kindness:

Whaaaaaaa!

❝ Why, just this morning as I was going to the library to do some extra homework, I found the younger brother of my best friend standing outside his house, weeping and terribly upset. He thought he'd been locked out and that the rest of the family had gone to the supermarket without him. Of course, I gave at least half my sweets to him, to cheer him up . . . ❞

" And then, of course, I bumped into the elderly man who lives down the other end of the street. He told me the story about how much he had enjoyed coconut mushrooms when he was a little boy so I simply had to forfeit the delight of eating them myself so that I could have the much greater pleasure of letting him eat them."

"There would have been some sweets left, which I would have enjoyed sharing with my cousin, except that a dog chased me and grabbed the packet from my pocket before I had a chance to stop him . . ."

CLEAN YOUR TEETH PROPERLY!

"If you ate so many sweets that you had to tell such a big fib, I'm surprised that you've got any teeth left! Are you trying to get into the Guiness Book of Records for eating the most sweets in the shortest possible time? You will, almost certainly, munch your way through another pile of chocolate bars on your own before the year is out – the temptation is bound to be too great. My advice is to pace yourself better through the calories and TO CLEAN YOUR TEETH PROPERLY!"

"Or try chewing on a nice piece of old sea rope."

Who Needs Excuses?

Nearly everybody needs an excuse for something at some stage — even the biggest goody two-shoes gets it wrong sometimes! So be on the look-out for other people who might try to make excuses to you:

* Your Dad, when he hasn't got enough cash to give you your pocket money.
' I spent it all on your goldfish.'

*Your Mum, when she's late picking you up from school because she was delayed at work.
'Well, when I was a child, I had to walk home on my own!'

*Your sister, when she's borrowed your mum's best jumper and spilt 'Vampire Blood' nail polish down the front.
'But it's hipper like that.'

*Your brother, when he's put his elbow through the kitchen window.
'I was killing a mosquito!'

*Your Gran, when she's forgotten your dad's birthday.
'I thought you were too old for things like that!'

*Your grandad, when he's forgotten your gran's birthday.
'But you look so young I didn't think you ever had a birthday!'

*The bus driver, when the bus is half an hour late.
'Don't blame me — blame the traffic.'

*Your friend, when her bus didn't turn up on time and made her late for ballet class.
'. . . and then three came along at the same time!'

*The weatherman, who promised sunshine and it rained.
'Well, at least it didn't snow!'

***The dinner lady, when she dropped
200 plates on the floor.**
'I had a smashing time!'

***The footballer,
when he scored an
own goal.**
'It was that end in
the first half.'

***The tennis player,
when she dropped
her racquet.**
'At least I didn't
drop my knickers!'

*The weightlifter, when he pulled a muscle.
'I think I've peaked my pecs!'

*Your best friend, when they forget they're going roller-blading with you.
'I was going so fast I went right past your house.'

*The pop singer, when he sang the wrong lyrics.
'I never liked the right ones anyway.'

The Sun has got his hat Hip! Hip!t Hurray!

*The cat, when she coughed up
a furball on the best rug.
'Tell me off and I'll scratch the armchair!'

AND DON'T FORGET!
Whatever the situation,
there is always one excuse
that is guaranteed to be
the ultimate:
**THE GOLDFISH ATE
MY KNICKERS!**

So, You Want to Stay Up Late?

Going to bed on time is something that mums, dads, grannies, grandads, lollipop ladies and teachers have a big thing about. Every now and then, they might, just, let you stay up a bit longer – but only because there is an educational film on the telly or because your aunty (and all your horrible spotty cousins) have come to visit you for the day. So, usually, if you want to stay up late you'll either have to be very lucky or very scheming . . .

Say, 'There are mites in my bed!' which will give your parents bedtime palpitations!

CLICK! CLICK!

CLICK!

CLICK!

But if you think they won't fall for that . . .

Try to stay awake longer than your parents. (This is never too difficult; parents are notorious for being exhausted most of the time, though nobody knows why.) Then, once you can hear them snoring, get out of bed again to play with computer games or whatever it was you wanted to do.

And, if all else fails . . .

Time for a TALL Story

Just as the grown-ups are about to tuck you up in your wincyettes, remember your special astronomy project for school. You know, the one where you have to wait up to observe the special equinoxical-hemi-spherical-quincentennial-eclipsical-shooting star-meteoritical wonder that can only be seen tonight? You explain that unless you do stay up to observe it, you'll be the only child in the school (in fact, probably, the only child in Europe) who will miss out. And your education will suffer for ever as a result.

"Honestly, you porky-pier! Even I've got to admit this one is quite clever. But what will you do when this meteoritical wonder isn't featured in the papers tomorrow?"

"Say you got the date wrong."

"Ok, smarty pants."

"I would be if you hadn't eaten them."

equinoxical . hemispherical . quincenta nnial . eclipsical shooting . star . meteoritical . wonder

37

No Cash and
Need to Dash?

Well, excuse me, but what's exactly new about that?
Since when did anyone of your age have any cash?
But you've still got some stuff you want to buy.
Some purchases simply can't wait until:

a) the next pocket-money day;
b) your birthday;
or
c) Christmas.

Don't say: '*My pocket money fell through the holes
in my pockets.*' Nobody will believe you. Your family
knows that you run out of money all the time.

Write your ideas for earning some money here:

Selling toys

How might you wheedle some money out of a grown-up? (They're all stinking rich.)

Getting it at night

A 'good cause' might come in handy. It could be time for a . . .

TALL Story

'The thing is, I'd really like to make a special surprise birthday/Christmas present for Aunty Nelly/my brother/my sister/you and dad. And, in order to make it, I need to buy some special equipment immediately. I can't wait until my next pocket-money day because I must start this extra-special, time-consuming present as soon as possible or it won't be ready on time. I'm afraid I can't tell you exactly what object I shall be lavishing so much loving care on – if I did, it would spoil the surprise. I am at your mercy – pretty please?'

"You TOERAG!* Fancy fibbing about wanting to spend money on other people when what you really want to do is spend it on yourself."

"Yeah – but it's always more fun to buy things for yourself."

"Like the Queen, I never carry any money."

*See page 19 for further explanation!

Sporting Blues

Does rugby make you rave? Swimming make you sick? Games make you grumble? Don't despair! You can give tennis the elbow with a cleverly-devised excuse. Here are some cunning suggestions for avoiding your least-favourite sporting pastimes:

Cross-country running: "I'm hiding from a group of talent scouts who'll ambush me as soon as I step out of the school gates and make me do a star appearance on *Top of The Pops.*"

Netball: "*My neck hurts.*"

Football: "*My big toe hurts.*"

Hockey: "*My stick's got woodworm!*"

Country Dancing (YUK!): "*But I'm tone deaf!*"

But don't, whatever you do, say:
"*I forgot my PE kit!*"

Sport Sickness

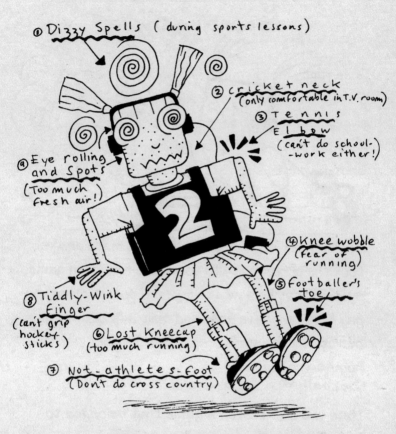

① Dizzy Spells (during sports lessons)

② cricket neck (only comfortable in T.V. room)

③ Tennis Elbow (can't do school--work either!)

④ Eye rolling and Spots (Too much fresh air!)

④ Knee wobble (fear of running)

⑤ Footballer's toe

⑧ Tiddly-Wink Finger (can't grip hockey sticks)

⑥ Lost Kneecap (too much running)

⑦ Not-athlete s-Foot (Don't do cross country)

Which is your least favourite kind of PE?

skipping

What could you say to avoid having to do it?

"My aneul hurts!"

Game for a Laugh?

Your brother went out with his best mate and you took the opportunity to touch the forbidden games system that he saved four years' pocket money to pay for. Now you've gone and spilt a fizzy drink all over it. Will you survive, once your brother comes home to find out?

Have you ever broken a game that belonged to someone else?

NO

What did you do?

NOTHING

"You could try being totally truthful, but even I have to admit that it might not get you very far."

"And do you really want to spend a month in hospital?"

OPTION 1: You could offer to pay back your brother so that he could buy a new games system. But if he took four years to save up for it, what hope have you got of saving the money in the next ten years?

Or. . .

OPTION 2: Tell your brother that you smelt burning in his bedroom and thought the whole system was about to go up in smoke – along with all his CDs, videos, posters and other precious things! You had no alternative but to pour the nearest liquid over the system – and that just happened to be some fizzy drink. You're sorry for the damage, of course, but think how disastrous everything could have been if you hadn't put the fire out!

⟨⟨*Still a tricky one. Nothing is going to pacify your brother in a disaster like this. If I were you, I'd try getting your mum or dad in to act as the mediator. I certainly wouldn't stay in the room with your brother on my own!*⟩⟩

⟨⟨*Have you tried running away?*⟩⟩

⟨⟨*You could always jump into the bowl with me!*⟩⟩

47

Homework Hassle

You admit that you haven't done your homework and the strictest, severest teacher in the school is about to tell you that you'll have to do one million lines plus the homework you should already have done by nine o'clock tomorrow morning. How will you get out of this one?

The dog was sick all over it at breakfast, so I'll do it again tonight.

What are your three best excuses for not doing your homework?

1 ....My Hamster ate it!....

2 ....I Lost my book bag!....

3 ....The rabbit scratched it!....

❝I could always try eating your homework — if you ever did any, that is!❞

Unfortunately, most teachers are so old that they've already heard every excuse known to school kids, so this situation demands an excuse which is so unbelievable your teacher might actually fall for it. Could be time for a **TALL** Story . . .

Why I Haven't Handed in My Homework
by I. De Lours

'I was sitting in my bedroom with my pencil poised to start the challenging piece of homework when there was a very loud bang outside. When I opened the front door, I found a silver-coloured man, about a metre high, standing on the doorstep. He was an alien from out of space who was looking for the nearest telephone. Apparently, his flying saucer had broken down and he needed to find a mechanic to help him get it going again.

Well, only the week before, I had read a book entitled Spacial Flying: How to Get Up there and How to Remain There, so I knew exactly what the problem was. The sumpmajolica

had seized with the borderlinka, which meant that the wingnutmini couldn't flow with the centripatum properly. This problem could not be sorted quickly without the aid of a spanneritoolius.

Unfortunately, we didn't have one

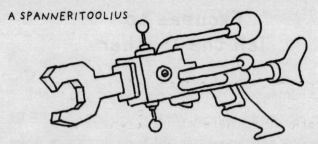

in our kitchen and the alien (whose name was Eric) wasn't carrying one either. Fortunately, the lady thirty-four doors-but-two down the road did have one and, after another hour or so, the flying saucer was up and whizzing again.

My mum and I waved goodbye to Eric and went back indoors. Just as I was about to start my homework again she said, 'But darling child, it's so late! You must be quite exhausted with all that hard work. Have an extra helping of chocolate biscuits and go straight to bed so you will be properly rested for school in the morning.' And my caring mother refused to let me stay up a moment longer.'

Excuses to Tell the Teacher

Horrible homework's not the only reason you might need an excuse at school. What if you left your PE kit at home? Or perhaps you might bung up the loo when you try an experiment with flushing conkers? It's always a good idea to have some instant excuses up your sleeve for emergencies. Learn these by heart – you never know when you might need them . . .

**"ANOTHER TEACHER CAME
IN TO BORROW IT!"**

"MY PARENTS WON'T ALLOW IT."

**"IT WAS THE ELEPHANT
IN THE PLAYGROUND."**

"IT ALL STARTED WHEN THE BOA CONSTRICTOR GOT OUT OF MY MUM'S BRIEFCASE . . ."

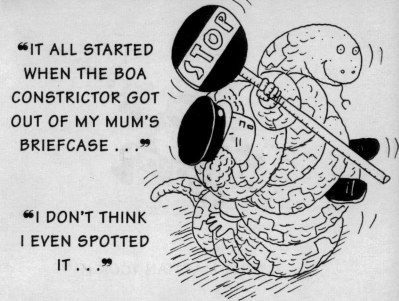

"I DON'T THINK I EVEN SPOTTED IT . . ."

"MUST RUSH – I'M OFF TO COLLECT MY PET TARANTULA FROM THE VET."

"BUT MISS, YOU SAID . . ."

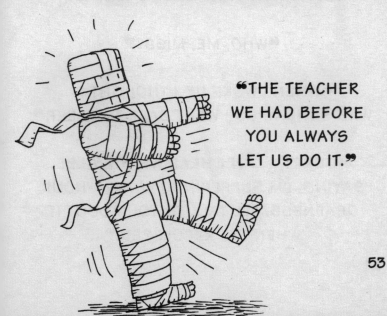

"THE TEACHER WE HAD BEFORE YOU ALWAYS LET US DO IT."

"THE MARTIAN TOOK IT!"

"HOMEWORK? WHAT HOMEWORK?"

"BUT I WAS CERTAIN IT WAS
WEDNESDAY THAT WE HAD MATHS."

"WHO, ME, MISS?"

"WHEN I WOKE UP, I THOUGHT IT
WAS SUNDAY, SO I WENT BACK TO SLEEP."

"SORRY, I CAN'T HEAR WHAT YOU'RE
SAYING, I'M SUFFERING FROM 24-HOUR
DEAFNESS. I'LL TALK TO YOU ABOUT IT
WHEN I'VE RECOVERED."

"OF COURSE I DID MY HOMEWORK MISS – BUT I LEFT IT ON THE BUS!"

"I KNOW THIS WILL SOUND INCREDIBLE BUT I'M ALLERGIC TO:

a) WRITING
b) CHALK
c) SWIMMING
d) GAMES

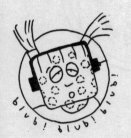

e) ....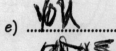

f) ....

g) ....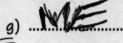

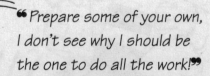

"Prepare some of your own, I don't see why I should be the one to do all the work!"

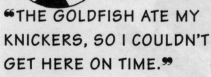

"THE GOLDFISH ATE MY KNICKERS, SO I COULDN'T GET HERE ON TIME."

"We've had that one before!"

"SIR – IS THAT CABBAGE OR A BOGEY ON YOUR JACKET?"

(You can say this for anything. It's not really an excuse but it'll certainly take his mind off things for a few minutes!)

Teacher's pet

School Report Blues

What's the worst thing that's ever happened to you at school? Write it down here.

My worst teacher is:

The subject I hate most is:

My worst school dinner ever is:

My excuse for not eating school semolina pudding would be:

All Stuck Up

Your parents have just bought a new sofa and you've gone and spilt glue all over the seat. There is smoke coming out of your dad's ears and your mum has gone purple before fainting. How are you going to get out of this sticky situation?

Glue? What glue? AH, _THAT_ GLUE!

What not to say:

"But I just wanted to see how far across the room you could squirt the glue from the tube."

You need to make your parents think you were doing something for someone else when the accident happened. Could be time (yet again) for a **TALL** Story . . .

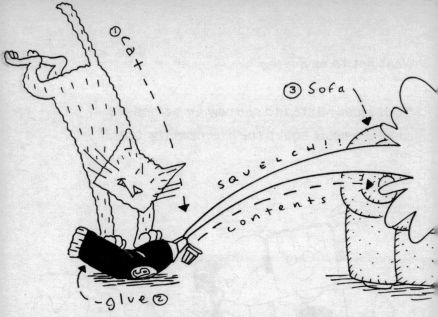

' I was about to make Granny the most amazingly unique birthday card. After all, she really likes it when I spend hours and hours making things especially for her. Just as I was about to glue something down, the cat jumped on the glue tube. The glue simply squirted out and went 'squelch' onto the new sofa. I really do feel very cross on your behalf and will go to the shop that sold the glue and complain about the faulty tube straight away.'

❝This is the point at which you make a quick exit.❞

Of course, Found U Out would say:

"Instead of doing my craft work on the table, which I had covered with a piece of protective newspaper, I was in a rush to get on with things and thought that I could make my card more quickly on the sofa. I realize now just how very silly I have been and can only offer my apologies. I shall forfeit my pocket money for as long as it takes to pay for the sofa to be cleaned professionally.**"**

Train for the Trainers!

How could your parents possibly imagine that you could be seen in broad daylight wearing last month's style of trainers? This calls for some drastic action.

But these ones stink – here sniff!

“That's enough to make anyone run a mile – ho ho!**”**

My other pair is totally worn out

(You'll have to prove this with hard evidence.)

Incredibly boring!

Really cheap!

Last week's style!

Totally
brilliant!

Really
expensive!

New
style!

Do not try saying:

a) But everyone else has got some (weak excuse)

b) You never buy me anything (bad move!)

c) If you get them for me, I'll do all the washing up, every day, for ever (no one will believe you!)

❝Another pair of trainers? And these new ones look so much like all the other pairs you've wanted and been given . . .**❞**

❝They're a slightly different shade of black.**❞**

❝Some of us manage without any shoes at all!**❞**

Green Greens?

Another happy family supper at which your mum is expecting you to eat revolting, smelly and soggy dark green vegetables again. They are so appalling to your taste buds that you can't even recognize them — except that they are *GREEN*! Can you avoid them being forced down your delicate throat?

But I can't eat these! They'll give me bottom burps!

Have you seen the latest report about how cabbage causes rapid brain-cell deterioration?

I saw the food hygiene inspector at the
greengrocers as I was going past this morning.

If all else fails, try a **TALL** Story . . .

'Good grief, mum! The whole world's gone green and
you don't even seem to be aware of it! Everyone else
has heard about the poisonous sprays that they put
on fruit and vegetables in the supermarkets these
days. Everything is sprinkled liberally with the stuff
so that it lasts longer on the shelves and still looks
green when it eventually lands on your plate. Don't
you care about the health of your family? Don't you
know how the whole world is thinking these days?
Honestly . . .'

"You should be ashamed of yourself for giving your mum such a hard time – it's just possible that she knows far more about pesticides and the green movement than you think. She might have cooked organic vegetables that haven't been sprayed. And what's more, dear child, if you don't eat your greens you won't grow up to be big and strong!**"**

"Who needs to be big and strong when you could be small, golden and perfect?**"**

Quick Excuses

If you're the sort of person who seems to make a habit of getting into trouble every day (and let's face it, who isn't?), then you ought to have some quick excuses at the ready to get you out of unfortunate situations — or at least to give you more time to think up a proper excuse. You could consider memorizing some of these:

SORRY — ARE YOU TALKING TO ME?

IT WASN'T MY FAULT!

PARDON?

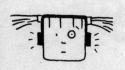  

I'VE NEVER SEEN
IT BEFORE.

I'VE NOT NOTICED
THAT PICTURE HAD A
MOUSTACHE DRAWN ON IT.

ARE YOU SURE YOU
DIDN'T SELL IT?

SORRY – I THINK THE
DOG'S FLUFFED!

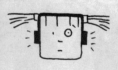

DID YOU PUT IT
SOMEWHERE ELSE?

I THOUGHT IT ALWAYS
LOOKED LIKE THAT.

I WASN'T HERE AT
THE TIME . . .

I COULDN'T POSSIBLY,
I'VE GOT MY HOMEWORK
TO DO.

WHY DO YOU ALWAYS
BLAME ME?

Why does everybody blame me ?!!

IT MUST HAVE GOT
LOST IN THE POST.

I PREFER MY TROUSERS
WITH STAINS ON THE KNEES!

I BLAME THE SHOP THAT SOLD IT.

HAVE YOU SPOKEN TO
THE MANUFACTURERS?

y bike wasn't like this before you borrowed it!

I blame the manufacturers.

NEXT DOOR'S PET LION
MUST HAVE EATEN IT.

IT WAS IN PERFECT WORKING
ORDER THE LAST TIME I SAW IT!

YOU LAUGHED THE FIRST TIME . . .

I WAS LEARNING MY TIMES
TABLES AT THE TIME.

BUT YOU WERE THAT UGLY
BEFORE IT HAPPENED!

IT WAS HIM.

IT WAS HER.

IT WAS THE DOG.

IT WAS THE CAT.

IT WAS THE GOLDFISH!

"Not again!"

And if none of these work — put in for a transfer!

End of Term Temper

So, it's the end of the summer term and you're zooming
home with a spring in your step because you've got
the long, hot, lazy summer holidays in front of you.
However, when you step through the front door, you
discover that your mum's hair has gone grey and your
dad's hair has fallen out completely! While you were
happily cleaning out your locker and singing the school
song at the end of year assembly, your school report
arrived. You collapsed in cookery, egg-flipped in
English, sank in science and mashed in mathematics.
Your parents are demanding an explanation:

I blame the government.

You do have several other options:

I D A
VO I D IT

I D A
VO I D IT

OPTION 1 This could be the ideal opportunity to tell your parents that there is a new pupil at your school who, quite amazingly, has exactly the same Christian name and surname as you. It is therefore highly likely that, at this very moment, this child is receiving all the high praise for the excellent school report that was destined for you! Oh, the injustice of it!

OPTION 2 Or perhaps this could be the moment to remind your parents that, had they bought you the brilliant new computer that everyone else at school has, you would, of course, have kept up with the rest of the class, and been ultra-brainy.

OPTION 3 You could inform your parents that, had you been given a decent amount of pocket money (rather than the incredibly stingy allowance you normally get) you could have purchased a decent pen. It would have enabled you to write more neatly, helping your teacher to read your handwriting properly and give you the high marks that your work justly deserves.

How am I supposed to do good work with this!

OPTION 4 Had you been permitted to watch more telly like absolutely everyone else at school, you could have learned so much from the educational programmes.

"A bad school report, eh? Do I detect an entire summer holiday of doing extra school work and going to bed early? I suggest that you buck your ideas up."

"Faced with an entire holiday doing extra work, I'd pretend to be busy doing something else, like a project."

"Or watching the telly, more like!"

Dodging Your Relatives

It's Sunday afternoon, and you're just settling down to a couple of hours with your fave computer game when your mum comes in, pulls out the plug and tells you to put on your smartest clothes. Yes, it's time to visit your ghastly relatives again. But don't despair. Here are some reasons for not visiting them this week:

Your swotty cousin
'I must stop at home to learn some quadratic equations and brush up on my scrabble technique.'

Your kissing aunty
'I'm suffering from an extremely contagious disease which can only be passed on through sloppy kisses.'

Your baby cousin

'The school nurse says I've got particularly delicate eardrums which are damaged by exposure to screaming.'

Your granny's best friend

'I'm allergic to mothballs!'

Your mad uncle 'I'm too young to die!'

"It's alright Ida! You'll only be a newt for a few moments!!!..."

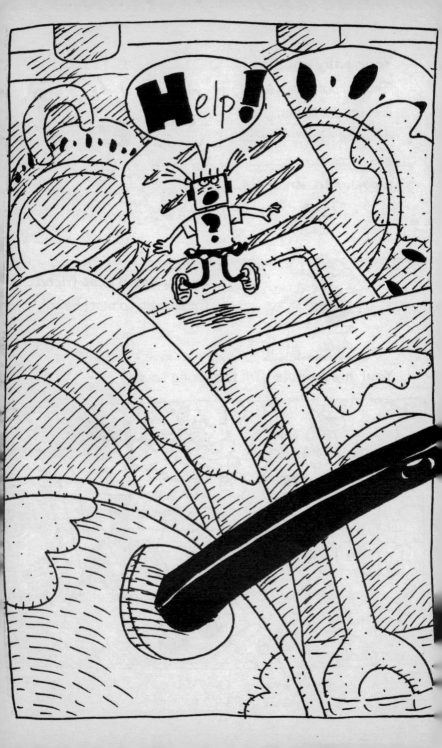

Waffle Disaster

SITUATION: There is an enormous pile of greasy, slimy and burnt pots and pans in the kitchen sink.

REASON FOR IT: You decided to try making waffles but didn't ask your parents' permission first. (Oh dear!)

OUTCOME: The mess has been discovered and your parents don't have a dishwasher. You must clean it up yourself, now.

Have you ever made a mess in the kitchen? What were you doing?

....

Were you found out? How did you clean up the mess?

....

The only solution in a waffle disaster zone might be a **TALL** Story . . .

TALL Story

'Well,' you say, 'it wasn't my fault. Making the waffles was part of our domestic science project at school. We had to do the practical at home because the entire school kitchens burned down last week. I got everything ready and followed the recipe exactly but, when it got to a crucial moment, I glanced out of the window and spotted next door's cat digging up the bulbs that you worked so hard to plant over the weekend. Without giving a second thought to my own domestic science marks (which contribute to my end of year report), I picked up the washing-up liquid, rushed out and squirted it at the cat to shoo it away. By the time I got back from rescuing the garden, my cooking was ruined.

I couldn't do the washing up because I'd now used up the last of the washing-up liquid. As I am only a young and delicate child, I don't have enough muscle power to scrub the pots clean — and, in any case, because they are all your best pots I knew you would want to make sure that you cleaned them carefully yourself.'

❝This is too much!

1   You've been cooking without asking permission to use the ingredients and having an adult there in case you started a fire!

2   You're blaming next door's pet for something it hasn't done. (What if your parents complain to the neighbours?)

3   You must have thrown away a perfectly good bottle of washing-up liquid in order to fulfil your excuse.

4   Why should anyone else clean up after your disastrous cooking attempts? It's outrageous!**❞**

❝Of course I'd help if I could, but I've only got fins.❞

Permanent Pause

Oh dear . . . a major boo-boo now. You've gone and recorded a cartoon over your dad's most favourite ever film on video!

Run for it!

But if your dad runs faster than you do . . .
This is a bad one – so, don't admit it! Hide behind the sofa! Claim to have been in Outer Mongolia at the time of the crime! Remind your dad that you are forbidden to programme the video recorder, so it couldn't possibly have been you – could it?

"Well, you must be the biggest coward I know! Why don't you just confess, you can always offer to rent the video from the library instead."

"Anyway, your dad probably likes cartoons as much as you!"

"Don't ask me, I'm only the goldfish around here, I have to watch what everyone else does."

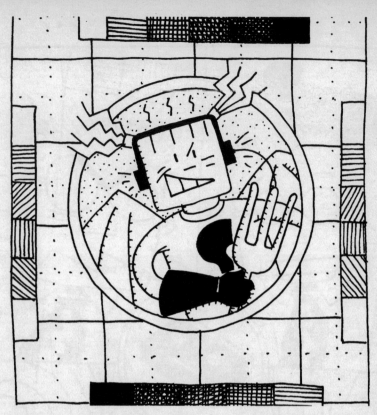

Have you ever recorded over someone else's video by mistake?

....

What did they say?

....

What did you do?

....

Video Nasties Report

My least favourite film is:

My least favourite children's programme is:

My least favourite TV personality is:

Programmes I'm never allowed to watch are:

The most boring programme on TV is:

Excuses to Tell Yourself

Now, if you're squeaky-clean honest, you'll admit that there have been times when you've done something that you really wish you hadn't. Perhaps you pinched your best friend's last sweet? Or you rang someone's doorbell and then ran away before they answered? Or you lumbered your brother and sister with the washing-up by pretending you had a test to revise for? The dangerous thing with excuses is, you might realize that you've started making them to yourself!

I WASN'T REALLY
HORRIBLE . . .

I COULDN'T
HELP IT . . .

HE SHOULDN'T HAVE
BEEN STANDING
THERE AT THE TIME!

BUT IT WAS REALLY FUNNY!

SHE LAUGHED AS
WELL LAST TIME . . .

IT WASN'T MY IDEA.

HE MADE ME DO IT!

I COULDN'T HELP BECAUSE
I WAS BUSY . . .

I COULDN'T HELP BECAUSE
I WOULDN'T HAVE BEEN
VERY GOOD AT IT.

IT WENT A BIT WRONG . . .

THEY JUST DIDN'T HAVE
A SENSE OF HUMOUR

THE WINDOW WASN'T IN
THE WAY LAST TIME . . .

IT WORKED WHEN THEY
DID IT ON TELLY!

IT WASN'T MY
FAULT BUT . . .

I BET SHE'D LAUGH IF SHE
WEREN'T SO OLD . . .

DAD WOULD UNDERSTAND
(if Mum tells you off)

MUM WOULD UNDERSTAND
(if Dad tells you off)

I COULDN'T BE BOTHERED

"Wouldn't it be best not to get into trouble in the first place?"

"Get real! Everyone does something wrong at some stage."

"Except goldfish."

"Except when they eat someone else's knickers."

93

I'M SORRY WE HAVEN'T FINISHED
THIS BOOK BUT. . .

"We ran out of ink!"

I'M SORRY WE HAVEN'T FINISHED
THIS BOOK BECAUSE:

"We had something better to do!"

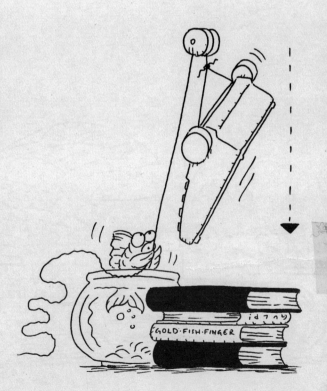

GOLD·FISH·FINGER

I'M SORRY WE HAVEN'T FINISHED THIS BOOK BUT. . .

"We thought somebody else had!"